P9-DGW-422

P is for Passport

A World Alphabet

Written by Devin Scillian

Illustrated by a collection of nationally acclaimed artists

*For my editor Heather Hughes, who opened
the door to a whole new world for me.*

DEVIN

Text Copyright © 2003 Devin Scillian
Illustrations Copyright © 2003 Sleeping Bear Press

All rights reserved. No part of this book may be reproduced in any manner
without the express written consent of the publisher, except in the case of brief
excerpts in critical reviews and articles. All inquiries should be addressed to:

Sleeping Bear Press
310 North Main Street, Suite 300
Chelsea, MI 48118
www.sleepingbearpress.com

Sleeping Bear Press is an imprint of The Gale Group, Inc.,
a division of Thomson Learning, Inc.

Printed and bound in Canada.

10 9 8 7 6 5 4 3 2

Library of Congress Cataloging-in-Publication Data

Scillian, Devin.
P is for passport : a world alphabet / by Devin Scillian.
p. cm.
Summary: A passport and rhyming text celebrate the author's adventures
discovering differences as well as similarities, from "A" for the variety of
animals that populate the planet to "Z" for the time zones that mark the
days around the world.
ISBN 1-58536-157-7
1. Travel—Juvenile literature. 2. Geography—Juvenile literature.
3. English language—Alphabet—Juvenile literature. [1. Travel.
2. Geography. 3. Alphabet.] I. Title.
G175 .S355 2003
910—dc22   2003015840

Here it is, come take a look.
    I know it's small. It's my favorite book.
It's filled with wonder, a wild adventure.
    It's called a *passport*, and here's the clincher—
it's a book completely written by me
    of the places I go and the things that I see.
        Each colorful stamp is a trip I took.
    There's a world inside my favorite book.

A a

Despite the extremes of weather and terrain, animal life is found almost everywhere on our planet. People are greatly outnumbered by animals. In fact, for every person on earth, there are some 200 million insects.

The largest animal on earth is the blue whale. Its tongue alone can be the size of an elephant. Whales eat plankton, which are among the smallest creatures on earth. Some animals are so closely associated with a certain country that it seems impossible to think of one without the other:

A panda from China.
A kangaroo from Australia.
A camel from Egypt.
A llama from Peru.

Illustrated by Gijsbert van Frankenhuyzen

An agile African ape, an antelope quietly grazing.
Alligators, ants, and aardvarks. It's all absolutely amazing.
An anaconda in the Amazon, an American armadillo,
an alpaca in the Andes as fluffy as a pillow.
A is for the Animals that climb and swim and fly.
They roam the bush in Australia and soar through an Asian sky.

A British boy in Brighton, eating a buttery bun.
Another boy in Brooklyn eats a bagel in the sun.
In Brisbane it's called damper. In Bordeaux it's a baguette.
It's a tortilla in Buenos Aires. Are you getting hungry yet?
From biscuits in Baton Rouge to naan in Bombay,
B is for Bread all over the world, baking every day.

Simply put, bread is cooked dough made from moistened flour. Just about every region and every group of people in the world have their own version of bread. Bread is a very old food, eaten since pre-historic times. Breads come in all shapes and sizes and an endless variety of flavors. They can be sweet or sour, crusty or soft.

A bagel is a round roll with a hole in the middle. A bagel is boiled before it's baked. Damper is a traditional bread in Australia. A baguette is a long, slender loaf of chewy French bread. Tortillas are round and thin and are often filled with other foods. Naan is a flatbread from India.

Illustrated by Gary Palmer

Bb

Many travelers like to collect coins and bills from the countries they've visited. You can learn something about a nation by the people and events depicted on its money. A good traveler has to know the "exchange rate" for the currency she carries. The exchange rate helps you convert one kind of currency into another.

For instance, if you're in Thailand and you know that there are 42 baht in an American dollar, then you know that a shirt costing 880 baht is worth about 21 U.S. dollars.

For many years, the nations of Europe used only their own currencies. But today, whether you're in Belgium, Spain, or Luxembourg, you can buy things with *euros*.

Illustrated by K.L. Darnell

You'll need a **C** for Currency, the money that you'll spend.
But whether it's *kroners*, *pounds*, or *rupees* will naturally depend
on where you are. You'll need to know when you make your travel plan
that it's *rubles* in Russia, *shekels* in Israel, and *yen* when you're in Japan.
Pesos in Mexico, *euros* in Europe, and in the U.S.A. you may holler
to know Australia, Canada, New Zealand, and Fiji all call their currency the *dollar*.

We're in Dakar and it's dreadfully dry, whipped by the sand in the breeze.
Or it's day in Death Valley, dangerously hot at 120 degrees.
A dazzling sun dries out the Gobi, a harsh and punishing land.
The largest on earth is called the Sahara, nine million miles of sand.
D is for Desert, the dusty dunes that almost never see rain.
But there's beauty and life hidden inside the sunbaked, desolate plain.

Deserts are the world's driest areas, usually getting less than 10 inches of rain in an entire year. And on the rare occasions when it does rain or snow, the moisture evaporates very quickly. Deserts cover about one-fifth of our world. Despite the harsh conditions, many plants, animals, and even people can make their homes in the desert. Only rain forests have a greater variety of life than deserts.

The enormous Sahara Desert stretches across northern Africa, while the Gobi Desert sits in central Asia. When you hear someone talk about the "outback," they're referring to the Great Western Desert of Australia. Both the North and South Poles are considered deserts because the only moisture is locked tightly inside vast plains of ice.

Illustrated by Katherine Larson

Mt. Everest stands 29,029 feet tall, the equivalent of nearly 20 Empire State Buildings stacked on top of each other. In a legendary expedition in 1953, Sir Edmund Hillary and Tenzing Norgay became the first climbers to reach the top. Climbing Mt. Everest is extremely dangerous even for experienced climbers. Over the years, many people have lost their lives trying to reach the peak. Climbers have to contend with thin air that is difficult to breathe, and wind, snow, and ice that can be fierce.

In Nepal, Mt. Everest is called *Sargarmantha*, which means "goddess of the sky." But in Tibet it's known as *Chomolungma*, which means "mother goddess of the universe."

Illustrated by Karen Holman

It won't be easy, this letter E. You may feel some hesitation.
Think of the energy and effort you'll need for this epic elevation.
Way up high, you'll endure the extremes of wind and ice and snow.
This is mighty Mount Everest with the entire earth below.
Half in Nepal, half in Tibet, you're up where jet planes fly,
on the tallest mountain in the world, five and a half miles high.

Temple of Heaven

Florence, Italy

Think of a cathedral in Florence, celebrating Christmas Mass.
Or find your way to the Christ of the Andes in the Uspallata Pass.
It's flowers at a temple in Bangkok. In Cairo, it's a Friday of prayer.
It's the flicker of fire and a Cherokee flute in the Oklahoma air.
F is for Faith felt by the followers of every religion and creed.
While we call God by different names, we're a faithful world indeed.

It is almost impossible to understand the people of other nations and cultures without understanding their faith. Spiritual beliefs are a powerful force in the way people live their lives and build their communities. A tour of the world's faiths might bring you Sikh prayer beads from India, a Hindu lotus flower from Nepal, a Catholic rosary from Rome, and a Shinto ema, or wooden plaque, from Japan.

The Christ of the Andes is an enormous statue of Jesus Christ that stands on the mountainous border between Argentina and Chile.

The western faiths of Christianity, Judaism, and Islam are monotheisms, which means they teach the presence of one God. Eastern faiths, such as Hinduism and Buddhism, focus instead on believers looking within themselves to find enlightenment.

Illustrated by Pam Carroll

Ff

You're sitting in Munich with a plate of dumplings, or in Tokyo with a bowl of ramen.
A platter of pasta, a breakfast of porridge. What do they all have in common?
They come from the world's most important food. That's why **G** is for Grain,
like Mexican corn, Moroccan couscous, or wheat from the Kansas plain.
And one more grain you'll find everywhere, prepared in many a way.
So important in China they ask, "Have you had your rice today?"

g G

Grain is the key ingredient in most of the world's diets. Grains are nutritious, inexpensive, and very versatile. For centuries, people have prayed for good weather and a good harvest because the success of a community's grain crop ensures the success of the entire community. Years in which the grain crop fails can be disastrous.

In many countries, grains symbolize prosperity. At weddings, rice is thrown at a bride and groom to wish them abundance. The Chinese word for rice is the same as the word for food. And the question "Have you had your rice today?" is asked in the same way that English-speakers ask, "How are you?"

Illustrated by Wes Burgiss

A horse farm in Halifax. A high-rise in Honolulu.
A house in Harare where they may be speaking Zulu.
A houseboat in Hong Kong, a Holland hotel.
A hostel in Hiroshima where young travelers may dwell.
A hacienda in Honduras, a historic hearth in Rome.
For all the places people live, H stands for Home.

Since the dawn of civilization, people have needed shelter for a place to live and raise their families. The homes people live in come in thousands of sizes, shapes, and materials, from enormous castles made of stone to cozy igloos made of snow. In many coastal cities of the world, people live on houseboats, or on homes that are built on stilts above the water.

A tour of the world would show you houses made of mud, adobe, straw, brick, canvas, wood, cement, metal, glass—almost every material imaginable. Some homes are built to last for centuries; others are torn down, carried to a new location, and built again.

Illustrated by Bruce Langton

Holland

Honolulu, Hawaii

H h

Some people think of Australia as an island since it is completely surrounded by water. But it is large enough to be considered a continent rather than an island. That means that Greenland is the world's largest island. Vacationers love to travel to tropical islands for vacations. Places like Hawaii, the Seychelles, and the many islands of the Caribbean are favorite getaways because they're sunny and warm all year round.

Easter Island in the Pacific Ocean is one of the most isolated places on earth. But travelers journey there to see the enormous (and mysterious) stone heads that sit along the island's coast.

1,400 islands make up the Greek Isles. The Isle of Skye is off the coast of Scotland. P.E.I. is shorthand for Prince Edward Island, the smallest province of Canada, and the setting for Lucy Maud Montgomery's classic book, *Anne of Green Gables*.

Illustrated by Mark Braught

I i

The Emerald Isle of Ireland. Or Iceland, surprisingly green.
I The chill of Greenland, the warmth of Tahiti and everything in between.
You'll need an I for Islands, such popular destinations,
many with beaches, lovely sunsets, and lush accommodations.
The Isles of Greece bleached by the sun, the lovely Isle of Skye.
Or follow the tale of *Anne of Green Gables* all over P.E.I.

J j

Some jungles are also known as rain forests. Rain forests are ecosystems that are incredibly important to the world's natural balance.

Rain forests are teeming with life. More than half of the world's species of plants, animals, and insects live in the rain forests. The canopy, or upper layer of a rain forest, can be so densely packed with vegetation that it can take 10 minutes for raindrops to reach the jungle floor.

Along with beautiful plants and flowers and a breathtaking array of animals, rain forests have many gifts for us. Many medicines come from plants found in the jungle. And because the plants of a rain forest breathe in carbon dioxide and breathe out oxygen, the mighty Amazon Basin has been called the "Lungs of the Earth."

Illustrated by Karen Latham
and Rebecca Latham

We're off on another journey and you jump at every sound.
It's all so dense and dark and there's wildlife all around.
It's steamy, hot, and humid, and you just might lose your way,
for you're trekking through a Jungle, and that's the letter J.
Watch out for jaguars and the spiders that may bite you,
but the parrots and the orchids will thoroughly delight you.

K Every traveler needs a K for a place to keep your stuff.
K is a Knapsack with plenty of pockets. You can never have enough.
You'll need a camera, a couple of pens, a bottle of water to sip,
a guidebook or two, perhaps a map, and a journal for recording your trip.
A first aid kit, and then you're ready for Kuala Lumpur or Tangiers.
Just make sure to leave some space for bringing home souvenirs.

A traveler needs to know a few things about his destination to prepare for a journey. Someone traveling to the Canadian Rockies in January will need to pack a warm coat, gloves, and a hat. But someone visiting Costa Rica in August will need shorts and sunscreen.

The right souvenir can help a traveler relive a journey for years to come. It could be a ticket stub for a ballet in Moscow, a menu from a restaurant in Toronto, or a disc of music from a musician in the Paris subway.

Photographs of your travels are a treasure, but remember that in many countries it's important that you ask for permission before taking someone's picture.

Illustrated by Pam Carroll

k

K

The most widely spoken language in the world is Chinese, or Mandarin. Twice as many people speak Chinese as any other language.

Some languages are only spoken in their home nation (like Finnish in Finland). But other languages are spoken in many countries. Arabic is spoken in dozens of nations from North Africa across the Middle East and into Asia.

English is an official language of more than 50 countries. They include the United States, Canada, Great Britain, and Australia, as you might expect, but also India, Kenya, the Philippines, and Zimbabwe.

In many languages, "good day" means "hello." The following are greetings in various languages:

shalom = Hebrew
kalimera = Greek
ni hao = Chinese
zdravstvuite = Russian
jambo = Swahili
bon jour = French
buenos dias = Spanish
guten tag = German
buon giorno = Italian
konichiwa = Japanese
al salaam a'alaykum = Arabic

Illustrated by Joanna Yardley

L l

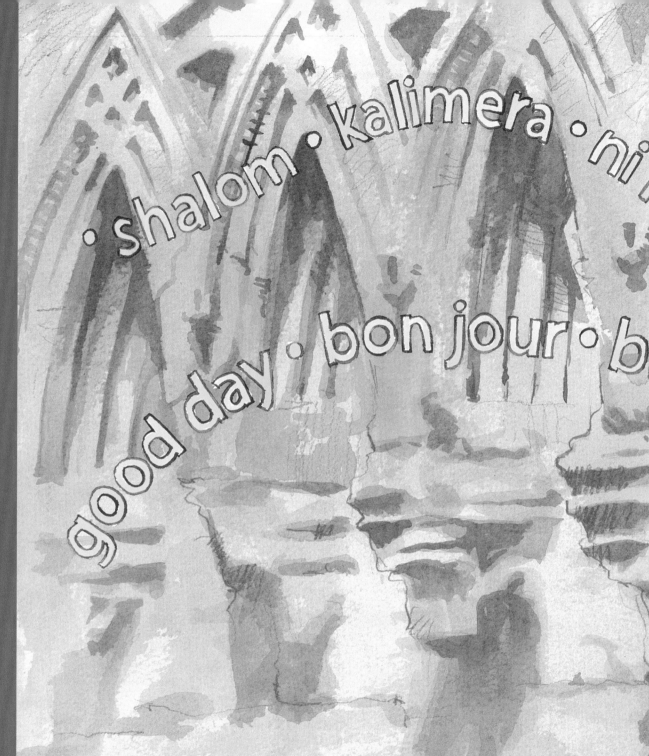

· shalom · kalimera · ni hao

good day · bon jour · bu

Polish is spoken in Poland. In Japan, it's Japanese.
    In Brazil they don't speak Brazilian, but rather Portuguese.
L is the long list of Languages, so many ways to speak.
Like English and Spanish, Italian and Hebrew, Arabic and Greek.
    So pack a handy phrase book and learn a few things to say.
A friendly "Bonjour!" or "Buenos dias!" can go a very long way.

A mountain mandolin, a marimba on the sand.
The Mexican maracas of a mariachi band.
It's opera in Milan in a most majestic hall,
or a group of string musicians on a street in Montreal.
M It's rock, it's reggae, it's whatever moves your feet.
is for the Music that gives our world a beat.

M m

Though you'll hear music just about everywhere in the world, some nations are famous for their native music. Travelers might want to hear reggae in Jamaica, salsa in Cuba, a symphony in Austria, an opera in Italy, or Celtic music in Ireland.

Some nations become famous for certain instruments. There's the didgeridoo from the Australian outback, a sitar from India, or a ukulele from Hawaii. The music can also be combined with a nation's native dance like the samba in Brazil or the tango in Argentina. But in the modern world, music can cross borders and boundaries with ease. You may hear American bluegrass in Germany, British rock in Japan, or Spanish flamenco in Denmark.

Illustrated by Alan Stacy

N n

For some regions of the northern hemisphere, a summer day seems to last forever. That's because the sun never sets. In northern Norway, for example, the sun stays up around the clock in June and July. On the other hand, the pattern is reversed in winter when entire months can pass in darkness.

The Northern Lights are also known as the Aurora Borealis. Streams of colorful light shimmer on the far northern horizon in nature's light show. In the Southern Hemisphere, the same effect is seen in the Aurora Australis, or Southern Lights.

Illustrated by Susan Guy

N Look on any compass and you'll find the next letter.
N means North and you'd better pack a sweater.
It's Newfoundland and the North Pole with its sunny Arctic nights.
It's a northbound train in Norway to see the Northern Lights.
Navigators know that no matter where they are,
they can always find their way when they find the North Star.

If you came to Earth from somewhere else, you'd think it rather clear
that most of Earth is the color blue. There's a lot of water here.
So O is for the Oceans that roll and roar and sway.
Seventy percent of our world is sea, from bright blue to dark steel gray.
So remember when you're on the beach, playing in the sand,
we live on little spaces where the ocean gives way to land.

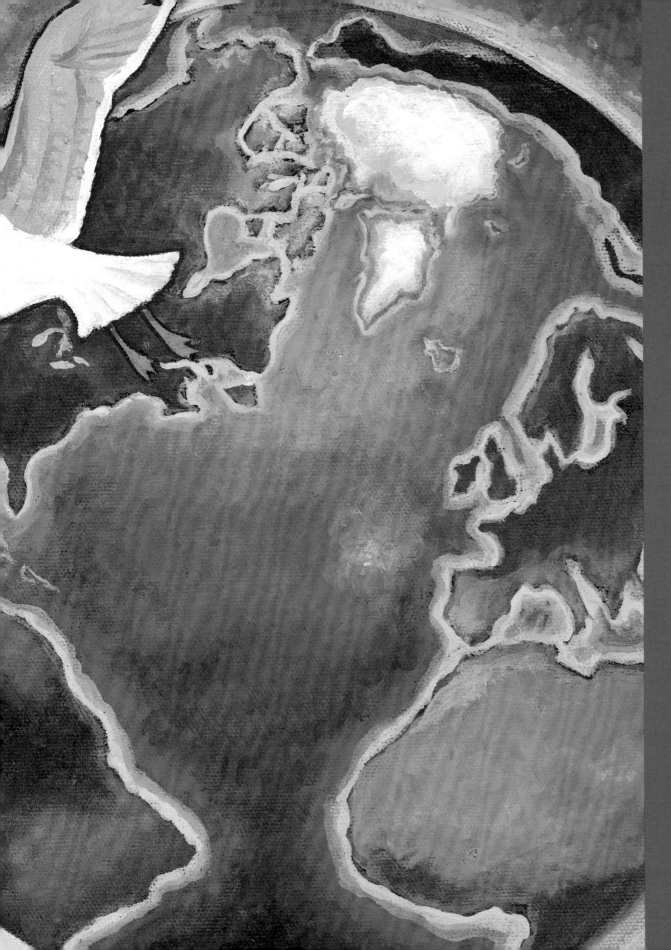

Oceans cover nearly three-fourths of the earth's surface. They hold 97% of the earth's water. The largest ocean is the Pacific Ocean, covering 64 million square miles.

Earth's longest mountain range is under water. It's the Mid-Ocean Ridge, which winds around the globe. It is four times longer than the Andes, Rockies, and Himalayas combined.

Because earth's oceans are so deep, scientists know more about the surface of the planet Venus than they do about the floor of our seas. It's believed there are millions of ocean species we have yet to identify.

Illustrated by Jeannie Brett

P is for passport, as you already know. But it's also for People, I've found.
Beautiful faces from so many places. People make the world go 'round.
They laugh, they eat, they sing, and they dance. They work, they sleep, they play.
They smile when they're happy, cry when they're sad, and teach their children to pray.
We wear different clothes over different skin, but it's always seemed to me
that with all of the things we have in common, how different can we really be?

Pp

More than six billion people live on the earth. Every year the number grows by another 100 million. The most populous nations on earth are China and India, both with more than a billion people. Think about it—there, if someone tells you that you're one in a million, it means there are a thousand people just like you!

While people have many similarities, there are many customs and traditions that are unique to certain countries. For a traveler, it's terribly important to learn them before traveling. For instance, it's considered rude to cross your legs while sitting in Thailand. The American hand gesture for "O.K." means "money" in Japan, Korea, and China. In Taiwan, belching after a meal is considered a compliment to the cook.

Special clothing can become a signature of a nation or a community, from the ornate beadwork worn by the Masai people to the colorful woven cloth favored by the people of Peru.

Illustrated by Gijsbert van Frankenhuyzen

Qq

Mount Kilimanjaro is the highest mountain in Africa. It's located in Tanzania.

For many years, people have searched Loch Ness in Scotland for the legendary Loch Ness Monster, but most experts doubt the creature actually exists.

One of the greatest construction projects in history, the Great Wall of China is more than 2,000 years old.

The Appalachian Trail is a footpath that stretches from Maine to Georgia.

With its beautiful ceiling painted by Michelangelo, the Sistine Chapel is part of the Vatican in Rome.

Australia's Great Barrier Reef is an underwater wonderland, the largest reef in the world.

Kissing the Blarney Stone in Ireland is said to bring the kisser the power of persuasion.

Illustrated by Helle Urban

The letter Q stands for quest, quests both large and small,
from climbing Kilimanjaro to seeing Niagara Falls.
Look for a monster in deep Loch Ness, or search for a giant blue whale.
Walk a while on China's Great Wall, or hike the Appalachian Trail.
Admire the ceiling of the Sistine Chapel, dig for a dinosaur bone.
Snorkel along the Great Barrier Reef, and kiss the Blarney Stone.

Say you want to travel from Riga to Rome, there's no need to fly or set sail.
You may want to ride as so many do, rolling along by rail.
R is for Railway, the tracks that can take you from eastern Russia to Spain.
For so many journeys the best way to get there is racing along on a train.
You'll rapidly rise right through the Rockies, or across the French Riviera,
or rumble across the Australian outback making your way to Canberra.

Train travel is the preferred method of travel in many parts of the world. It can be a marvelous way to see a nation's countryside while at the same time mingling with travelers from many other places.

On a train, you can tour the Canadian Rockies on the Rocky Mountaineer, travel the Scottish Highlands on the Royal Scotsman, race across India on the Royal Orient, or see Europe on the legendary Orient Express.

The world's longest train route is the Trans Siberian Railway from Moscow to Vladivostok, Russia. The journey takes six days.

Illustrated by Ted Burn

Here's a Sydney sailor, racing on the sea, a Spaniard spelunking in a cave.
Here's a Swiss skier, schussing down a slope, and a Samoan surfing on a wave.
It doesn't matter where you go, in Shanghai or Saint Tropez,
you'll find that people everywhere have lots of games to play.
S is for Sports, as we kick and jump. We skate, we throw, we run.
Sometimes it's a serious competition, and sometimes it's just for fun.

S s

The most popular sport in the world is soccer (known in many nations as football). Sports can be a great reason to visit other countries.

You might venture to Chile to go whitewater rafting.

You might travel to Austria to ride a bobsled.

You could head to Scotland to play golf in the game's birthplace.

Every four years, the athletes of the world gather to compete in the Olympic Games. Held in both winter and summer, the games symbolize the unity and friendship that can be created in sports competition.

Illustrated by Melanie Rose

T t

Since the dawn of recorded time, people have felt a need to explore. Many years ago, a traveler didn't have to go very far to find new lands and new people. The next village could feel like a whole new world. Gradually, travelers covered longer and longer distances and each new discovery created a desire to see even more—mountains, oceans, islands, the poles, and, eventually, outer space.

Whether you're visiting an exotic land on the other side of the world or a new neighbor on the other side of town, you're building a bridge for someone else to travel one day.

Illustrated by Rick Anderson

T Something happens on every journey as each new map is unfurled. That's why T stands for Travel, for travel can save the world.
You see, each trip a traveler takes is a moment that you spend getting to know a whole new world. And that world becomes your friend.
One day you think back to that café in Rome, or that night on the Waikiki shore, and you'll take better care of this marvelous world in a way that you didn't before.

Brazil is home to one of the world's largest cities (São Paulo), one of the world's most beautiful cities (Rio de Janeiro), and one of the world's most important rivers (the Amazon).

New Zealand is the only country to have every type of climate in the world. And in 1890, it became the first country to allow women to vote.

Australia is the only nation to occupy an entire continent.

In general, the temperature swing between summer and winter is not as dramatic in the southern hemisphere as it is in the northern hemisphere. That's because there is much more ocean in the southern hemisphere, which helps moderate temperature swings.

Illustrated by Jane Monroe Donovan

Our world is like a bunk bed; it has a top and bottom.
And when the top is having spring the bottom has its autumn.
U Most folks live in the northern half. Any map makes that clear.
But U is for Under, way down under in the Southern Hemisphere.
Australia, South America, New Zealand, too, and let's be more specific.
Part of Africa, Indonesia, and the islands of the South Pacific.

So you think our world is set in its ways, that it's hardly ever changed?
Then you should know it's just not so. It's constantly rearranged.
Deep in the earth, it's quite a scene, like a battle being fought.
Gases burn, lava churns, and it's bubbling, boiling hot.
So V is for Volcanoes, sending sparks and lava flows.
Each eruption means a change in the way our planet grows.

Deep in the earth's core, rocks melt into a red-hot liquid called magma. Sometimes the magma forces its way to the surface, creating a volcano. When the magma erupts and spills out of the earth, it's called lava.

There are more than a thousand active volcanoes in the world. The largest active volcano is Mauna Loa in Hawaii. Much of Mauna Loa is under the ocean. From its base at the bottom of the sea to its tip, Mauna Loa is actually taller than Mt. Everest.

The flow of lava and the spray of fire from volcano eruptions can cause many problems, threatening plants, animals, people, and homes. But the soil left behind from an eruption eventually becomes very rich soil for plants and animal life.

Illustrated by Ross Young

W means the Wonders of the World. They can wow you or move you to tears.
Some are quite ancient and thus they've inspired travelers for thousands of years.
Whisk away to Giza in the desert of Egypt where pyramids are waiting to greet you.
Or climb past the clouds of southern Peru to the city of Machu Picchu.
It's Big Ben in London, the Arch in St. Louis, the majestic Taj Mahal.
The Statue of Liberty, and the Eiffel Tower, wonderful wonders all.

WORLD MAP

You'll run out of travel time long before you run out of world wonders to see. The list goes on and on.

The Colosseum in Rome.
The Temple of Angkor Wat in Cambodia.
Stonehenge in England.
The Leaning Tower of Pisa in Italy.
The city of Petra, carved into the rocks of Jordan.
The Sydney Opera House.
The Grand Canyon in Arizona.
Mount Fuji in Japan.
The Golden Gate Bridge in San Francisco.

Illustrated by Maureen K. Brookfield

Xian and Xinjiang are just two of the **X** cities in China. There's also Xiamen, a beautiful city by the sea.

Like China, Mexico has many cities that begin with the letter **X**, like Xala, Xico, and Xalisco. X'cacel is a beach in eastern Mexico.

Xinguara is a city in Brazil.

Xenia is a city in Ohio.

Xenophobia is a fear or hatred of foreigners. It can cause many problems in a world full of people who often need to rely on each other.

Illustrated by Laura Knorr

We hardly use the letter X, but if you go to China one day,
you'll need it to go to Xian and Xinjiang, though the X sounds more like a J.
But to find yourself in Russia, Bolivia, or Ethiopia,
you'll need to leave one X at home, and that's for "xenophobia."
Xenophobes have a fear of those from foreign lands.
And they miss out on all the things a traveler understands.

Allillanchu

cama'i

Whenever you travel and take a trip, just remember while you're gone
that as you're moving and adding up miles, so is the world you're on.
The entire earth is a hearty traveler, always on the run,
making a journey through outer space, racing round the sun.
Y And it's constant travel, no time for stops, no time to hit the brakes.
So we'll let Y stand for Year, which is how long each trip takes.

Y y

The earth travels in several different ways. First, it rotates on its axis. It takes one complete turn every 24 hours, which equals one day. We don't feel it, but the earth spins at a speed of nearly 1,000 miles per hour.

We talk about the sun "rising or "setting," but we really mean that the earth has turned into or out of the sunlight.

Like the other planets in our solar system, the earth revolves around the sun. It takes 365 days for a complete revolution, which equals one year. Again, we don't notice, but the earth races around the sun at an amazing speed of 64,000 miles an hour.

Illustrated by Ginny Joyner

The letter Z is most important when counting the hours you've flown.
For when you travel you'll need to know exactly which is your Zone.
A time zone, that is, for when you fly from one part of the world or other,
you'll need to change your watch or clock as you move from one zone to another.
When it's noon in New York, it's evening in London, and just try to understand,
it's already tomorrow in Sydney, Australia and Yokohama, Japan.

Scientists created the world's time zones in 1884 after deciding that the world needed a uniform way of telling time. As if slicing a giant orange, they divided the world into 24 "slices" or time zones.

The times zones begin at the Greenwich Observatory in England, which is known as the prime meridian. Halfway around the world from there (or 12 time zones), you'll find the International Date Line, which marks the change between today and tomorrow.

Covering 17 million square miles, Russia is the largest country in the world and includes 11 time zones.

Illustrated by Helle Urban

Z
z